Eyes to See

Eyes to See

a 30 day prayer journey

Tiffany Nardoni

Contents

Introduction

No one has ever seen God; but if we love one another,

God lives in us and his love is made complete in us.

1 John 4:12

I long to have eyes that see people the way Jesus sees them. Why is it so difficult to love people well? I struggle with this deep, genuine kind of Jesus-love. I realized I just don't know how. Typically when we fear something or find something difficult, it's a lack of knowledge. So I asked myself, *do I really believe that we are all created equal? created in the image of the Almighty God?*

I can easily love my husband, my kids, my family, my friends. I am even pretty good at loving other people's kids. Or so I thought.

I thought I was praying this prayer, digging deeper into seeing people through Jesus' eyes because I struggled to show love to strangers and neighbors and acquaintances. But once I started praying this prayer, I realized how much I have to learn about loving the people right in front of me. I realized how much I miss the mark on loving my family. I realized how much I long to have love seep through my language, my response, my tone. I realized that it's mine for the taking, I only have to ask.

And once I started praying this simple prayer, my eyes will never unsee the things God has revealed to me. I have a long way to go in this journey of loving people well. And God will take every opportunity I give him to teach me more, to make my heart more tender, to lead me back to the cross and hopefully take others with me along the way.

Thank you for joining me in this journey. I pray that your eyes are opened to see people the way they are meant to be seen, as dearly beloved children of God. Blank pages are included at the end of every day. Please feel free to use these to journal your own journey, to write notes or prayers or questions, or even names of people you are led to pray for. This whole book is black and white, including the cover. I pray as your eyes are opened wide to those people God has placed in your life, the pages are filled with beauty, names and stories of your own.

Tiffany

The Beginning

God planted the seed for this book in 2015. He placed in my heart this prayer, this passion, this idea. I'm a slow learner, I guess. But what I've learned from the time it's taken to put all of this into place is this: there is no time limit on lessons learned from God. There is no right or wrong or competition. There is no such thing as checking it off my list. Growing in God, being sensitive to his whispers, listening to the Holy Spirit's leading, is just one yes after another. It's going deeper in the same lesson time after time. It's a journey.

I've always understood we won't reach perfection here on earth, but at the same time I think in my mind, maybe even subconsciously, I think I shouldn't have to learn the same things over and over and over again.

But, practice. And imperfection. And messing up and giving in and succumbing to my own selfish desires always puts me back to the place of being humbled before our Almighty Lord. The place of falling to my knees in awe of his patience and forgiveness and grace.

I pray that this is a blessed part of your journey. A part that will take you deeper and bring you closer to our Lord. I hope that as you spend just a few minutes for the next thirty days reading this, that you find yourself more in love with Jesus and the people He created.

This is what I wrote on my blog in 2015.

> *Lately I've been praying for eyes that see like Jesus. I want to see people for what they are; created by God, loved by him, desired by our Lord to be fully his.*

> *I am humbled. I am humbled because he has created in me a heart for others that I have only longed for in the past. I love my family intensely. That is so easy for me. I can even love other people's children pretty easily.*

> *But, strangers? Homeless? People that have been deeply hurt? Or worse yet, people who have hurt others? Things that I may see as too great a sin to love. Or maybe they've hurt me? They've dug a hole and somewhere inside me I've decided they deserve to live in it.*

This isn't so. And it's more than humbled my being. They hurt. They feel. They need Jesus and love and acceptance. Just like I do. Just like my kids do.

One day I realized I no longer turned away, I found myself praying for people with sad eyes. I found myself humble to the point of realizing it's not what they've done, it's what they are choosing to do about it. It's not what's been done to them, it's living in the freedom of putting the past behind us. It's about living in the hope of Christ.

My prayer circle has broadened to include more than just the helpless, innocent children, the fatherless, the orphan, the hurting. My heart now sees more deeply into the souls of the people around me, because Jesus created them. His heart hurts for his children.

When one of my children hurts a sibling, my heart aches. I am broken that my own child chose to hurt someone who loves them. I am saddened because they really should be looking out for each other. I am even angry because they did no control their actions. I am aching because one of my children is hurting.

How much more does God feel this for us? Each time we think a bad thought or say something nasty or purposefully offend someone, I can almost feel the sinking feeling in God's heart. Why must you hurt each other?

But as sad as I am when one of my children hurts another or disobeys, I never stop loving them. I am ready to hold them, hug them and go on with life. But we deal with it. We confess. We are broken. We forgive.

As parents, we see good in our children, but we also see them at their worst. And yet, we still love them. We fight for them. We'd do anything for them. It's a fierce kind of love that doesn't exist in many relationships. It's set apart and special. And it's a beautiful picture of the way the Lord loves us. There's discipline and guidance and free choice. But there's also forgiveness and mercy and grace.

When my adopted children (finally) come home, I do not expect them to love me. I don't really expect them to like me every day. But I want to see them through his eyes. I want to love them like Jesus loves them.

I want to pray for those around me who are hurting, but not in a generic way. In a way that is attentive and loving. In a way that my children might understand God loves us all and we all need him desperately. In a way that when my children hurt each other, they are willing to forgive. In a way that doesn't lose hope for healing.

So I pray that you can see people through his eyes. Because we are all beautifully created in his image. We are all sinful. We can all choose forgiveness. We can all choose Christ.

The Prayer

A few years ago the Lord laid it on my heart to pray for eyes to see people how God created them to be. Not the way they are or the way I think they are supposed to be. Not who they have become or who they were once. But seeing people with Jesus eyes. seeing people for who they are in Christ, with Christ, in the beginning with him. Not the sinful beginning of their birth. But the beautiful beginning of Creation. How we are all supposed to be.

And once Jesus opened my eyes to this, there was no turning back.

I began to see the woman at the grocery store, a lonely widow, as a child of God.

I saw the beggar on the street as a son of the Almighty.

I saw the misbehaving child as a dearly loved babe of our heavenly Father.

I saw the scantily dressed girl as a daughter of the Most High.

I pushed it away though. What am I to do? How I am to change these people's lives? I don't have time for them. It's dangerous. I don't have money to give. It's irresponsible. I don't have energy to spare. They know better anyway. I mean, right? These are (mostly) grown adults. They have to figure this out for themselves. We've all had to do hard things at times. I mean, right? Right? God?

You know that unsettled feeling in your heart that you get so desperate to get rid of? Ignoring it typically works after a while. Conviction, we'll call it finally gives way to less heavy things. Helping a neighbor paint a fence. Check. Making a meal for a new mom. Check. Visiting lonely people. Check. While these things are all good, we are called to have more than a servant's heart. We are called to love deep. We are called to endure. We are called to reckless abandon of these earthly things. We are called to bring glory to God above all things in all that we do.

There is no excusing it or denying it or waiting until the kids are grown and the time is right. We have no excuses. We are only to see these people as lovingly created by our good and sovereign God.

Here's my challenge for day one. Pray this prayer. Simply pray to see people the way God created them. It will change the way you see people. You will smile more. You will have more grace. You will love deeper. You will reevaluate your priorities. He will be faithful to answer. Because that's how God is.

Dear Lord,

I praise you for who you are and who I am becoming. I thank you for creating. You are a creative God. A faithful God. A humble God. As I am becoming more like you, dear Lord, I want to honor you in all I do. In how I live, Lord, I want to bless your name.

God, I pray that you would give me eyes to see. To see the hurt and the needs. To see your beauty and your suffering. And Lord, most of all, today I ask that you would begin to transform me. Open my eyes. I want eyes to see people for who you created them to be, not who they have become. I want to be like Jesus to the hurting people. And first I must see them the way you do, as dearly loved children belonging to an everlasting, always loving God.

In Jesus name, amen.

The Foundation

Now that I've introduced you to the prayer that changed my vision, the inspiration for this book, I want to go back. I want to go back because without a proper foundation of truth, this prayer could very well be

empty words. We must always begin with our own lives, in our own hearts.

We must know who we are, whose we are, in order to see others the way God created them. We must first see ourselves the way God created us to be. We must rest in being his. We must trust that we are his beloved, before we will ever love others as his. We must know full well, who we are created by and for. We have to let it cover us, that we are his children, dearly loved and made for a purpose. The purpose of glorifying our Creator. The purpose of love. To be loved. To accept love. To give love.

Do you believe you are his beloved?

Do you believe that Jesus came to earth for you?

Do you believe that Jesus died on the cross for you?

Do you believe Jesus rose from the grave, conquered death, for you?

You are so loved.

You are so loved by Love itself. You are worthy because of him. You are beautiful because of him. You are loved because of him. And you can love because of him.

Child of God, dwell here for just a minute. Rest here and whisper out loud. *"I am a child of God. I am beloved. I am created with love and for love because of Jesus."* Let's visit some truth.

So God created mankind in his own image, in the image of God he created them; male and female he created them.

Genesis 1:27

This righteousness is given through faith in Jesus Christ to all who believe. There is no difference between Jew and Gentile, for all have sinned and fall short of the glory of God, and all are justified freely by his grace through the redemption that came by Christ Jesus.

Romans 3:22-24

You see, at just the right time, when we were still powerless, Christ died for the ungodly. Very rarely will anyone die for a righteous person, though for a good person someone might possibly dare to die. But God demonstrates his own love for us in this: While we were still sinners, Christ died for us. Romans 5:6-8

Whoever does not love does not know God, because God is love. 1 John 4:8

If you are unsure of where you are with Christ. If you want to know more about a personal relationship with Jesus. If you are hungry to understand what this kind of love is all about, please stop here. Right now, just reach out to someone who has gone down this road before you. Find a friend. Email me - tiffanynardoni@gmail.com .

Pray. He will hear you. He is waiting for you to ask him. That's all it takes. Ask him to come into your heart, change it, and fill it with love. Enough to cover your mistakes and enough to give love away.

The Beckoning

A s I continue to pray this prayer to see people the way God created them to be, I begin to think more of people's souls rather than their bodies or personalities. I begin to see more eternal rather than temporal. My eyes are transformed and I cannot unsee it.

> *"You don't have a soul. You are a soul. You have a body."*
>
> *- George MacDonald*

God is using this simple prayer to change the way I see people, all people. I begin to be more aware of the souls of not only the ones I love, but of strangers. Even strangers I may never speak to or see again. Because I am praying this prayer, to see people the way Jesus meant for me to see them, the way they are created, the way Jesus sees them. I begin to hurt for them. A deeper aching for people's souls that creates in me a longing to show them Jesus.

Here's what I realized though. In praying this prayer I do see people as children of God. I see them for who they are meant to be, who they truly are, *beloved children*. Jesus beckons them to come to him. But not all of them know this. Not everyone accepts that they truly are children of the Most High God.

And so here I am, achingly continuing to pray this prayer. And I understand so much more of what Jesus feels. I feel it, too. The aching, the longing of his children to come close. The beckoning.

He beckons me, too. He wants me near. I feel his faithfulness. I wonder why he doesn't just save people. And he reminds me why we were created.

To glorify him.

It wouldn't glorify him much if we were all forced into trusting Jesus. It wouldn't glorify him if our choice was taken from us. We glorify him when we choose him over and over again above all else.

See what great love the Father has lavished on us, that
we should be called children of God!

1 John 3:1

As we continue to pray this prayer throughout this book, I pray you will be able to grasp the beautiful gift, the sacrifice, the love that God has for us.

My challenge for you today is to pray for those you see. Pray for these people, made in the image of God, to know him. To respond to the beckoning. To hear his call. To trust in Jesus. As you pass a stranger, pray. As your eyes meet that frazzled mama, pray. As you pass the person jogging on the sidewalk, pray. The beggar, the daycare worker, the gas station employee, the neighbor, the person with the flat tire, your insurance agent. Say a simple, one sentence prayer for them.

Lord, I pray they know you more today.

For this reason I kneel before the Father, from whom every family in heaven and on earth derives its name. I pray that out of his glorious riches he may strengthen you with power through his Spirit in your inner being, so that Christ may dwell in your hearts through faith. And I pray that you, being rooted and established in love may have power, together with all the Lord's holy people, to grasp how wide and long and high and deep is the love of Christ and to know this love that surpasses

knowledge- that you may be filled to the measure of all the

fullness of God. Now to him who is able to do immeasurably

more than all we ask or imagine, according to his power that is

at work within us., to him be glory in the church in Christ Jesus

throughout all generations, for ever and ever! Amen.

Ephesians 3:14-21

Gentle Shepherd

Lord, help me to see people the way you created them to be.

I pray this prayer and my eyes are forced open. Not a harsh forced opening, a gentle forced opening. Like a father leading his child, God is leading me into this unknown.

Lord, give me eyes to see people the way you see them.

And suddenly, forcefully, gently my eyes are wide open. My children. My children are *his beloved.*

He's placed these precious souls into my care. I am entrusted with their lives. I am to guide them, guard them, love them, serve them, teach them and let go of them. Let them go into his arms. His care. His direction. And he leads through me. And yet I find myself…

short tempered.

annoyed.

expecting perfection.

answering harshly.

lost.

wandering.

wondering.

questioning.

The Lord knows my mama heart. I never intend to be this short with them. My children are gifts, blessings. I love them with all my strength. Yet I fail them. Because I am human. And the Lord knows this, because he also created me. And he knows me well. He knows us all well. He knows my children well.

So with tender heart, I step back. Take a breath. Observe them. I am watching their movements and interactions with each other.

A gentle answer turns away wrath, but a hard word stirs up

anger.

Proverbs 15:1

Do they reflect how I treat them? Are they mimicking me? *yes.*

Is this how I want them to treat each other? Is this the value I have placed on them? Do they know they are beloved? By me and by God?

This unknown. Here I am. I am the shepherd guiding my flock. Their hearts are being molded by my words. Their souls are being fed by my leading. But I feel I go at this blindly. How do I love them well? How do I teach them to see themselves and others as God has created them to be? *Beloved.*

Dear one, you are beloved. Beloved by me and our heavenly father. He is our gentle Shepherd. Thank goodness I am not alone. We are in this together. We are learning together. You mimic me as I learn from our Father. Here we are, pressing forward.

I am not always all the things listed above, but I long to be more of Jesus to the ones I am to lead. As I go through each parenting day, I pray that he makes me more like him. I pray for eyes wide open to see my children for who they are created to be, *his beloved*. Each with different ideas and personalities and interests and quirks. Each made in the image of God, our creator.

I allow them to talk and I will listen. That much our Father has taught us.

I allow them to stray and I will lead them back. Again, our Shepherd shows us the way.

My eyes are opened now. They are his children. And I am more of Jesus to them…

patient.

interested.

forgiving.

gentle.

sure.

steadfast.

understanding.

attentive.

because he is more to me. The more I open my hands and heart and let him in. The more he remakes me as a parent. The more he guides my words. The more I can hear his gentle whispers of wisdom.

Thank you, Lord for showing us the way. You are our gentle Shepherd. We don't need to look far or wander. You are here. Always. Always guiding and leading and listening. Thank you, Lord for always being near.

He tends his flock like a shepherd:

He gathers the lambs in his arms and carries them close to

his heart;

he gently leads those that have young.

Isaiah 40:11

Deeper

Dear Lord, as we pray this prayer, take us deeper. Take us into the unknown. Shine your light into the dark places of our hearts. Help us to see more of you in our everyday. Help us to see people the way you created them to be, as your beloved.

Journeying deeper into the Lord's heart. Here we are, standing with open hands and tender hearts. He moves within our souls to draw us closer to himself. He sheds light into areas that were once too dark to see. He never leaves us alone. And together we press on into this hard place of loving well.

Now that you have purified yourselves by obeying the truth so that you have sincere love for each other, love one another deeply, from the heart.

1 Peter 1:22

Today, Lord we pray this prayer again. And today Lord, you ask us to replace interruptions with opportunities.

As we go about our day today, we pray for opportunities to love people. God will bring people into our paths, with open eyes we will see them.

When we are tempted to rush on, I pray we pause to say a prayer.

When we are tempted to brush off, I pray we stop and listen.

When we are tempted to say no, I pray we ask the Lord first.

When we are tempted to get frustrated at unwanted delays, I pray we choose to see the joy in the moment.

When we are tempted to lose focus, I pray we set our minds to Christ alone.

When we are tempted to close off and shut out, I pray we move forward with tender hearts.

Whatever interrupts our plan for the day, Lord, I pray we remember it's your plan not ours. Your ways are not our ways. And we trust you, Sovereign Lord. We trust you with our time, our days, our schedules, our interruptions. We trust that you will show us how to see the opportunities when we would normally see set backs. We trust you, Lord for wisdom and peace. We trust you Lord, for tender hearts and sensitive souls. We trust you, Lord, to take us deeper. We trust you, Lord, to guide our day.

"For my thoughts are not your thoughts, neither are your

ways my ways," declares the Lord.

Isaiah 55:8

You will keep in perfect peace those whose minds are

steadfast, because they trust in you. Trust in the Lord forever, for

the Lord, the Lord himself, is the Rock eternal.

Isaiah 26:3,4

But I trust in you, Lord; I say "You are my God." My times are

in your hands;

Psalm 31:14,15a

One Another

I saw you today, dear mama. You were wrestling a toddler in the grocery store. You looked frazzled and you yelled. You glanced around to see if anyone was watching.

I've been there before, mama. I've barely held it together in the store just to get out the door. I've bit my tongue until it came unglued in the car. Then I've yelled. I've let them know just how disappointed I was, how angry. I've made empty threats. I've cried burning tears. I've said things that I can never take back. I've tried anything and everything to convince them to obey. And I've failed over and over again, exasperated, defeated, feeling so very small.

I'm sure someone saw me, too. I hope it was someone who prayed for me. Who understood me. Who remembered what it was like to be in that place.

So often though, we forget. We fail each other. We see with only our eyes instead of our hearts. And we miss it big time.

Today when I saw you, our eyes met. I smiled a little. I wanted to tell you that today is just a good day for my kids.

They are following me around like little ducklings, but that's not always the case. They are quiet and well-behaved. But sometimes they aren't. Sometimes I feel like I'm failing. Sometimes I am terrified at the choices they might make as they grow up. Sometimes I'm the frazzled mom in the grocery store wrestling four big kids and a baby. Sometimes I don't want to make eye contact with the moms around me because I'm slightly embarrassed that my child won't take no for an answer.

(I've also asked for forgiveness…a lot. I've had to apologize…a lot. I've had to learn to hold my tongue…a lot. And I've had to pray for wisdom and self-control…a lot. Because our kids deserve that kind of mom.)

But, you see, as I've been saying this prayer, with open hands, to our Lord, I see people deeper. I don't see a mama wrestling a toddler, I see a child of God struggling to breathe deep the goodness of the Lord. I see his beloved hoping not to be judged but to be loved. I see you, a person created in the image of God, dearly loved. I see God's heart longing to be close to you.

I think I'm beginning to scratch the surface of this Jesus' eyes thing. I think he is answering my prayer. I think there is so much more he has to offer.

Jesus, give me eyes to see people the way you see them.

Love one another.

As I have loved you, so you must love one another.

John 13:34

The Beggar

I f I lay the bare bones of my heart out there, I'll tell you

that I try not to see your eyes.

I pass the beggar on the side of the road.

Because who am I to help?

Because I have young children.

Because there are places for them to go. To find help. To eat

food.

Because they have lost their own way.

Because they must find a way back again.

Because I don't trust them.

Because I don't believe them.

Because I am afraid.

Because I have mouths to feed, too.

Because I am in a hurry.

Because I don't want to.

Bare bones, heart truths. This is where my mind goes. Yet I am no different than a lonely beggar. I am dirty and lowly and as much of a mess. I am the beggar.

Who am I to make these calls? Who am I, with full belly and soft bed? Who am I, with clean water and clothes to spare? Who am I to say I shouldn't give?

Because if the Holy Spirit prompts me to give, I am to give open-handed, whole-hearted, fully, genuinely all of me. I am not to care what they do with it or whether they need it or if they are being manipulative or deceitful or lazy. Nope. Not my call.

My job is to obey. I am not telling you to give food to the man on the side of the road or to whittle away your life savings to every person who asks. I am saying that to us, as believers in Christ Jesus, as believers in eternity with Jesus, that we are first and foremost to obey the Holy Spirit's leading.

And if he leads us to give, we give. If he leads us to stop, we stop. If he leads us to speak, we speak. If he leads us to make eye contact, to say a prayer, to simply say hi, then we do it. Because we are all beggars. We are all human. We are all created in the image of God. We are all his masterpieces.

Keep on loving one another as brothers and sisters.

Do not forget to show hospitality to strangers, for by so doing some people have shown hospitality to angels without knowing

it.

Hebrews 13:1,2

Today, I pray that you are near enough to hear the Holy Spirit's gentle whisper. I pray that your blind eyes can see the human being in the beggar. I pray that in humility we all come like the beggar to the foot of the cross. This is where we need to be.

Lord, make our blind eyes to see people the way you created them to be

.

The Undoing

Lord, give me eyes to see.

How could I have known offering up these meager words would cause the blind to see?

I was, I am still, so blinded by my own thoughts, ideas, expectations and experiences. I hold onto what I think I know. I get caught up in the chaos of life. I busy myself. I plan, organize and fill up all my white space.

As I continue this journey, my eyes are opened wide. I have found that a cluttered life blinds me. This journey of seeing people the way God created them to be leads me into more unknowns. Taking me down unexpected paths, I find myself wanting more. And less.

More of God. More of time with him. More of real relationships. More of the deep. More of intentional conversation.

Less of the cloudy, scattered time with friends. Less of the rushing around, feeling stressed out. Less of the anxiety building up in my chest, ready to burst. Less of being on the outside looking in. Less of wishing I had time for more.

This prayer has undone me. I continue to pray this prayer because I don't learn something just once. This prayer will be a continual undoing of everything my flesh tells me to be. Of everything this world tells me I deserve. Of everything I practiced for so long.

Here I am, Lord, send me! But what if the Lord sends me right back to the place I was set out to leave? He calls me to hold loosely the things of this world. He calls me to hold tightly to eternity. He calls me to himself. And he calls me right back to this place. This place of letting go and holding on. This place of blind faith. All of these things he calls me to so I can finally see. I can finally see people the way God made them to be.

I only wish this was a lesson learned, something to check off the list and move on. But this seeing people as beloved. This undoing of all I've learned about loving people. This real Jesus-love for others, this will be journey. A journey of failing and getting back up again. A journey of seeing and turning away. A journey of apologizing and forgiving. A journey of serving and sacrificing and going to the uncomfortable place, just to be Jesus to them.

Just to be Jesus to them. Just to be "little Christ's", image bearers, believers, followers, children of the One True King.

My challenge to you today is to pray this prayer again. Ask Jesus to help you to see people the way they were meant to be, not how they are or who they've become. But as beloved children of God. And step back, take a breath. Maybe you are a chaos coordinator like I am. Maybe you are a to-do lister, get the job done type person. Maybe you are like me and you need to tell yourself to make eye contact with people. You have to remind yourself to smile and say hi. Maybe you are like me, you need to slow down and breathe in the love of Christ today.

What is cluttering up your life today?

How can you make space to love people well?

When I ask this I am not asking for some crazy sacrifice. Let me tell you what this looks like in my own life:

I thought loving people was hard. It was hard to make the space or find the time. I thought it meant a huge commitment on my part.

Here's what I've found though, loving people well can become a habit. It's intentional. It's a group effort. It's a choice.

I've decided in order to love people well, I have to de-clutter my home. Minimalist lifestyle for the win! We are not completely "minimalists" but we are trying to be purposeful with what we own and what we do with our time. There was a lot of undoing here. But making this space and setting these boundaries has allowed us to spend more time with people.

And how can we love people if we aren't around them?

So, how are you going to love people well today?

And let us consider how we may spur one another on
toward love and good deeds,
not giving up meeting together, as some are in the habit of
doing,

but encouraging one another -

and all the more as you see the Day approaching.

Hebrews 10:24,25

This is my command:

Love each other.

John 15:17

The Least

I want you to know, I am an adoptive mama. It's important to me to share this. And if you ever see a photo of my family, it's pretty obvious. I'm just saying, it's no secret. My kids were old enough to remember when they came home. They were old enough to remember what it was like not to have a mama tuck them in at night. They were old enough to remember what it was like to see other people have daddies cheering them on. They were old enough to be afraid. And they were old enough to be brave.

In the culture they came from they were truly seen as the least. The least of all society. Frowned on, looked down upon, cast out. Most people could not understand why we would go so far, invest so deep, spend so much and sacrifice so hard to bring two children into our family.

It's not because we can't have biological children. I carried four babies full term, delivered them, held them and called them my own. They look more like other members of my family than myself, but they are mine.

It's not because it's easy. Sometime we can have a ten-course meal and talk about that. (Because that's how long it might take to share our adoption story.)

It's not because it makes us popular. Um, no.

It's not because it's cheap. Quite the opposite in fact. When we sit down to talk about "easy" we'll also go over "cheap". And I can also tell you how God provides in big ways. And small ways. And unforeseen ways.

We chose adoption because it's a beautiful testament of what the Lord has done for us.

We chose adoption because it's actually pretty easy for us to see children the way God sees them, as beloved. I know that's not the case for everyone. Some people still cannot understand how deep the love goes even when they never shared womb-space. I'm not saying adoption is for everyone, but I'd be lying if I said that I didn't believe orphan care was for everyone.

Lord, give me eyes to see people the way you created them, as dearly loved children. As beloved. As chosen.

Today as you pray this prayer, I hope that you enter into his presence with open hands and tender heart. I hope that you can pray for the orphan, the fatherless, the abandoned, the least of these, because that is caring for them.

Today I am asking you to pray for the fatherless. I am asking you to pray for them to know Jesus and to feel loved. I am asking you to pray not about what you can do or if you are supposed to adopt. I am asking you to pray for the orphan hearts, their souls, their minds. I am asking you to pray not because they are close to my heart, but because they are close to God's heart. It is not my choice to pray for these children, it is my duty. This is how we care. This is how we love. This is how we see them for who they are created to be, as beloved children of the King.

"…because when you pray for someone so much,
you can't help but love them."

I wish I could tell you who said that, but it was said to me about my own family when my son was in the hospital. So we'll go with a generous, loving, praying anonymous person. But it's so very true. Try it. I dare you.

Religion that God our Father accepts as pure and faultless is this; to look after orphans and widows in their distress and to keep oneself from being polluted by the world.

James 1:27

A father to the fatherless, a defender of widows, is God in his holy dwelling.

Psalm 68:5

Unbelief

Why do we as Christians hold unbelievers to the same standards we   hold ourselves to?

Or maybe you don't. But I'm pretty sure I did for a long time. Maybe I still do sometimes.

Once I started praying for eyes to see, I realized just how blind I was. I was blinded by my own experiences, my own ideas, my own expectations. I was blinded by my own "goodness".

Yet, I never claimed to be perfect. I never thought I knew everything. I just simply weighed my sin against theirs. I never did the really big, the really bad things. I didn't really *hate* anyone.

But did I *really love* them?

When I asked myself this question and really let my heart speak…I was silent. And embarrassed. And ashamed.

Because maybe I didn't hate people. Maybe I didn't do anything to hurt them. But maybe I didn't do anything to love them, either. And maybe that's just as bad.

I suddenly felt like the lukewarm believer. And it all made sense to me.

Instead of going about my day not harming others (and also not pushing myself out of my comfort zone) maybe I should go about my day pursuing others. Pursuing Love. Pursuing Jesus.

Maybe I should go about my day loving the people right in front of me. Maybe I should go about my day with eyes wide open, seeing the people that God places in my path. Maybe I should pray for people to be placed in my path.

Loving people begins by noticing them. Saying hi. Taking cookies to a neighbor. Sending a text when they pop into your mind. Pausing your day to listen. Trusting in the Lord enough to put that to-do list on the back burner and sit with a hurting friend.

Now instead of gasping at sin (how could they…? why would they hurt someone so badly…?) My eyes are opened because hurt people hurt people. Lost people wander. Sad people seek fulfillment. And all people, believers and unbelievers, need Jesus. Over and over again, we need him. Over and over again, we fail. Over and over again, we must choose Christ.

And isn't it my own unbelief if I doubt that people will change? Isn't it my own unbelief if I don't allow God to use my own life to love others boldly and bring them to himself? Isn't it though?

Dear Lord, we pray for eyes to see. Lord reveal to us the lostness of the ones around us. Help us to see them as wanderers looking for hope and answers. Lord, remind us we hold the answers. You have given us a spirit of power and love and self-discipline. Make us bold. Make us humble. Give us tender hearts and gentle words. Help us to bring others to the foot of the cross with us. Help us to live love. Lord, give us willing spirits and open hands. We come to you for all your power, all your wisdom and all your love. It overwhelms our souls and fills our hearts to overflowing. You are good, God. Show us the way. Light our paths. We want to live for you. Help our own unbelief. We lift our hands to you, Lord. Take our lives as a living sacrifice. We long to love you well. Amen.

For the Spirit God gave us does not make us timid,

but gives us power, love and self-discipline.

2 Timothy 1:7

Therefore, I urge you, brothers and sisters, in view of God's

mercy, to offer your bodies as a living sacrifice, holy and

pleasing to God- this is your true and proper worship.

Do not conform to the pattern of this world,

but be transformed by the renewing of your mind.

Then you will be able to test and approve what God's will is

-his good, pleasing and perfect will.

Romans 12:1,2

Come As You Are

Come as you are, friends. Gather around my table. Pour out your heart as I pour out the coffee. Bare the deepest parts of your soul as we unashamedly cry out and ask the Lord, *why*. Or *what*. Or *when*.

Come as you are, dearest friend. As we wonder aloud what God has in store. If the answer is no, then what now? Lay it down. At my table, at the cross. Lay down your heavy burden. Together we go before the Father. Together we longingly wait. Together we bow our heads, lift up our cries, beg for answers and bless his name.

There was a day when I wanted to have it all together. There was a day I thought I would get to a place where I was ready with all the answers. There was a day I foolishly looked forward to all the projects being complete, all the dishes being washed, all the laundry being folded. I kept telling myself once I got to this place then I'd have more time for people. Once I checked off my list, I could sit down and relax. Once I clean up, clean out, organize, paint, or plan all the things, then my life will be settled and I can invest in people. I thought people needed a person who was put together, knowledgeable, an expert on all things God with an abundance of wisdom and life experience.

Guess what? That was a lie. The truth is, we make time for what's important to us. The truth is, we will never arrive. The truth is, God doesn't expect perfection. God doesn't only use missionaries or pastors or teachers or scholars or theologians. He uses moms and wives and daughters and friends. He uses the sunrise and the sunset. He uses preschool teachers and writers and aspiring authors. He uses dish-washers and dinner-cookers. He uses baby-rockers and boo-boo kissers. He uses me and you and our children and our husbands.

As I pray this prayer, I invited them in. All of them; the weary, the burdened, the sad, the lonely, the hungry, the confused, the believer, the unbeliever. Come as you are. You are beloved.

But how can I ask them to come? How can I ask them to drop the facade? To stop pretending we have it all together? How can I ask them to come to my table, drink coffee, pour out their hearts? Isn't it better to cry together rather than cry *to* someone? Eyes to see = empathy. I am a sinner, lost and alone. You are a sinner, lost and alone. But, *Jesus.*

He came. He died. He rose. He saved. He continues to save. This whole refining process of being sanctified, being saved, being his. This whole life is a journey of being. Being with Jesus.

Come as you are. I'm here, too. Together we bring our burdens. Together we lay it down. Together we reach for him. Together we rise above the to-do list, the check list, the expectation. Together we bow down at the feet of the One who lifts us up.

Open your home, your arms, your heart to someone today. Invite them in, just as they are. Just as you are.

Come to me, all you who are weary and burdened,

and I will give you rest.

Matthew 11:28

No one has ever seen God; but if we love one another,

God lives in us and his love is made complete in us.

1 John 4:12

Forgive

I could sum everything up I need to say with this: forgive because we have been forgiven.

love because we are loved.

Praise the Lord, my soul;

all my inmost being, praise his holy name.

Praise the Lord, my soul,

and forget not all his benefits-

who forgives all your sins and heals all your diseases,

who redeems your life from the pit

and crowns you with love and compassion,

who satisfies your desires with good things

so that your youth is renewed like the eagle's.

The Lord works righteousness and justice for all the

oppressed.

He made known his ways to Moses,

his deeds to the people of Israel:

The Lord is compassionate and gracious,

slow to anger, abounding in love.

He will not always accuse,

nor will he harbor his anger forever;

he does not treat us as our sins deserve

or repay us according to our iniquities.

For as high as the heavens are above the earth,

so great is his love for those who fear him;

as far as the east is from the west,

so far has he removed our transgressions from us.

As a father has compassion on his children,

so the Lord has compassion on those who fear him;

for he know how we are formed,

he remembers that we are dust.

The life of mortals is like grass,

they flourish like a flower of the field;

the wind blows over it and it is gone,

and its place remembers it no more.

But from everlasting to everlasting

the Lord's love is with those who fear him,

and his righteousness with their children's children-

with those who keep his precepts.

The Lord has established his throne in heaven,

and his kingdom rules over all.

Praise the Lord, you his angels,

you mighty ones who do his bidding,

who over his word.

Praise the Lord, all his heavenly hosts,

you his servants who do his will.

Praise the Lord, all his works,

everywhere in his dominion.

Praise the Lord, my soul.

Psalm 103

I wish it were so easy. Simple, yes. But easy, no. Although our minds know it's just that black and white, our hearts tell us all the gray. It gets so fuzzy here, guys. Like we say the right words but do we live them?

Today, are you living forgiven?

Eyes to see…the forgiveness in our own lives.

Eyes to see…the forgiveness in our friends lives.

Eyes to see…the forgiveness in our spouse's life.

Eyes to see…the forgiveness in our children's lives.

Eyes to see…the forgiveness in our enemies lives.

Are you living free? Are you forgiving others because He forgives us every single time? Are you forgiving yourself? Because Jesus doesn't ask us to live in the shame, he tells us to live in the freedom of forgiveness for the things we've done or not yet done. Because he did the once-and-for-all thing of dying and raising from the dead. He was beaten and bruised for *us*. He went through torture and agony, for *us*.

Lord, we pray for eyes to see your forgiveness in our own lives. Help us to accept this truth and live free in you. Lord, we ask for eyes to see forgiveness for others. Help us to see them as your children, fully free, fully forgiven. And Lord, help us to understand how to treat each other this way. God we long to fully comprehend this act of forgiveness. We long to do this well. We know you will teach us how, lead us well, love us hard.

In Jesus name, amen

To forgive is to love. To love is to forgive. I love how the psalmist talks about how short our lives are in the same breath he talks about God's everlasting love and forgiveness. Life is too short to waste our days on vengeance or anger. Our days are numbered, our breaths are few. When I look at how I spend my days I want more of loving others and less of knocking them down. More of building them up, pointing them to Christ and less of making them doubt. I want to spend more time smiling, making eye contact and mending relationships and less time avoiding or speaking ill of others. Make your day count today. Pray with me for eyes to see. Pray with me for a complete understanding of forgiveness. Pray with me for freedom to love others with abandon.

Rest

This need for rest runs deep, Lord. I never knew. My busyness kept me from knowing you well. My busyness kept me from loving them well. My busy mind, my checklist, my unsettled heart, my striving.

I cannot cease to strive. I cannot cease to do all the things; feeding my family, bathing children, cleaning up spills. But I can strive to rest. I can strive to know you more. I can strive to *rest in you.*

I wonder if I am even the same person I used to be. I know, Lord, I have changed. So was that truly me back then? The one with the giant list and the color-coded calendar? The one with the chores-must-be-done and house-must-be-perfect mentality? The one who wanted to do all the crafts and complete every task? The one who did it all…alone? And then stressed and yelled and did nothing less than freak out on the ones I longed to love the most? Am I even that same person?

Lord, who am I? This girl needing rest…

This rest. Rest. Commanded rest. Rest in Him. Rest in You. Rest in Jesus. Lay it all down. Turn it over. Give it up. Sabbath. Holy. Sacred. *Rest.*

I passed over this command for so many years. Prayed the prayer to "turn it over". Asked the Lord for wisdom, but in reality I think I wanted more time. More time to try harder, to succeed. The harder I tried, the more stressed I got. The more behind I got, the more out of control I felt. I worked so hard and this vicious cycle continued and it ate away at me. It stole my family time, my peace, my contentment. Those moments I will never get back, but the Lord is good. I have eyes to see this now. Where I was once blind to this need, in fact trying to fix it by doing the exact opposite of what I needed, I am now keenly aware of this void in my life. This hole that I once filled with all.the.things. I now fill with rest.

Rest that may not look like rest in your life. But rest, nonetheless. Rest that quiets my soul and calms my mind. Rest that pours peace into our home. Rest that is holy, unfiltered, sacred. Rest that is God. God is…a whole lot of things. He is more than I can comprehend. And somehow in his perfect plan, he made us with this deep desire to connect with him. For communion. For quiet. For peace. For companionship. For rest.

He knows that we cannot do this life alone. He knows it is over-whelming and too much. He knows what will fill the void in our lives and it isn't more things to do. Or getting all the things done. It's Him. It's rest. It's giving Him the worries, the fears, the burdens. It's blessing his name whether he gives or takes away. It's understanding our control is just whether or not we give him our junk and rest in his sovereignty or we strive to fix and finish and busy up our lives, always trying to arrive.

My days are short, numbered are my breaths. I will rest in him.

Just like I tell my children not to worry, it's not their job. Just like I want to take care of them, the Lord longs to take care of us. We are his beloved. Rest well, my child. I remind myself of this as I whisper it to my little ones. Rest well, your tired bodies. Rest well, weary souls. Rest well, my beloved.

Come to me,

all you who are weary and burdened,

and I will give you rest.

Matthew 11:28

The Lord replied,

"My Presence will go with you,

and I will give you rest."

Exodus 33:14

Yes, my soul, find rest in God;

my hope comes from him.

Truly he is my rock and my salvation;

he is my fortress, I will not be shaken.

My salvation and my honor depend on God;

he is my mighty rock, my refuge.

Trust in him at all times, you people;

pour out your hearts to him,

for God is our refuge.

Psalm 62:5-8

My Child

Here I am twelve years in to this whole parenting thing. I've prayed for my children before they were born. I have cried for them, prayed over them and given them up to the Father. I have loved them deep. I have hurt when they hurt. I have been moved to tears just watching them grow. I have lamented birthdays and rejoiced in milestones. I have sacrificed and served. I have messed up and asked for forgiveness. I have apologized, retracted, promised and gone out of my way a million times for my kids. I have lost sleep and my heart has swelled with pride. I have dropped them off places, told them they are brave, fought for them and had to let them go. I am a mama. I've been through the ringer. I've had biological babies, miscarriages, adoptions and child loss. I won't stop loving them no matter how much it hurts or how hard they push.

But it's not enough, that crazy mama love. The one that brings out the claws and pulls them into a cocoon. The one that defends and protects. Yes, that precious fighting mama love that God gives us the moment we realize we are mothers, is not enough. I have failed my kids a million and one times and I'm not about to stop there.

I listen to them speak to each other. I hear myself in them. I am short with them, impatient. I am condescending sometimes. I expect a lot from them. My tone of voice is their tone of voice. When suddenly you realize the very thing you are getting on to them about is the very thing they mimic in you. And you are not mimicking our Heavenly Father very well in that thing.

That thing may not be tone of voice for you. But I'll bet there is at least one thing left wanting. The Bible tells us so much about the strength of our tongue.

A gentle answer turns away wrath,

but a harsh word stirs up anger.

Proverbs 15:1

The soothing tongue is a tree of life,

but a perverse tongue crushes the spirit.

Proverbs 15:4

Oh, Lord, I don't want to be a spirit crusher! The ones I love the most will see the very worst in me. The ones I spend my life serving and protecting and praying for and growing into godly young people, are the ones that reflect my own failures, my own heart.

Dear Lord, we pray that we will begin to reflect your heart, not our own. We pray for your words to fill our mouths, your tone to set our day. Lord, give us eyes to see these children in our care. Help us to see their needs. Help us to point them to you, to mold their hearts and fill their souls. Help us to raise up warriors for you, gentle servants, godly men and women. Lord, thank you for entrusting us with these precious gifts. Amen

Creation

As I become unblind, the colors of the earth unfold. The beauty it holds is a reflection of our good God. But how often do we pass on by, eyes glued to screens or the checklist or the road ahead? How often do we rush through? Hurry on with heads so full? In the back of our minds we justify our actions, some day there will be time for this…when the children are grown, when summer comes, after Christmas, when we retire. When the bills are paid, when we are ahead, we are just scraping by, so busy.

Life shouldn't get in the way of living. Living with eyes wide open to the colors of creation, the sounds of the earth, the smells of the seasons, should never be a privilege but a right. A gift, a blessing. Fully alive in the Lord's creation is how we were made to be. Fully embraced in his love for us. Enveloped in nature. His handiwork surrounds us, we are free to rest in the palm of his hand, as his masterpiece.

His masterpiece. Of all of creation, we are his masterpiece. His most prized piece of artwork. Our creative Creator, our perfect Life-Giver, our servant King, our majestic, all powerful, gentle, Sustainer of life…created us to bring himself glory. Of all of the beauty of all of creation, we are the most beautiful to him.

From the summer skies to the autumn trees, from the pure white winter snow to the spring blooms, we are so much more precious to him.

Creation speaks his name. Conception whispers his praise. The breath in our lungs sings to an Almighty God.

Dear Lord,

Open our eyes today to all of your creation. When the world around us seems to crumble, Lord help us to slow down. To breathe in. To close our eyes and listen for your gentle whisper. In the bird's song, in the wind's breeze, in the leaves crunching beneath our feet. Lord, help us to feel your arms around us today. Help us to relish in the fact that you created us. Teach us to know full well we are your masterpiece. We long to live our lives as a living sacrifice, glorifying you in all we do. When we step out into your creation, Lord, remind us to step into your presence. We invite you in. To embrace us. To draw us close. To hold us tight.

Mold us into who you want us to be. Open our eyes, Lord, not only to see other people through your eyes, but also ourselves. Help us to see people the way you intended them to be, created in your image. We praise you with our voices, with our movements, with our breath. Thank you, God, for giving us eyes to see.

Amen.

In his hand is the life of every creature

and the breath of all mankind.

Job 12:10

For you created my inmost being;

you knit me together in my mother's womb.

I praise you because I am fearfully and wonderfully made;

your works are wonderful,

I know that full well.

My frame was not hidden from you

when I was made in the secret place,

when I was woven together

in the depths of the earth.

Your eyes saw my unformed body;

all the days ordained for me were written in your book

before one of them came to be.

How precious to me are your thoughts, God!

How vast is the sum of them!

Were I to count them,

they would outnumber the grains of sand-

when I awake, I am still with you.

Psalm 139:13-18

Lord, our Lord,

how majestic is your name in all the earth!

You have set your glory in the heavens.

Through the praise of children and infants

you have established a stronghold against your enemies,

to silence the foe and the avenger.

When I consider your heavens,

the work of your fingers,

the moon and the stars,

which you have set in place,

what is mankind that you are mindful of them,

human beings that you care for them?

You have made them a little lower than the angels

and crowned them with glory and honor.

You made them rulers over the works of your hands;

you put everything under their feet:

all flocks and herds,

and the animals of the wild,

the birds in the sky,

and the fish in the sea,

all that swim the paths of the seas.

Lord, our Lord,

how majestic is your name in all the earth!

Psalm 8

Blind

Oh Lord, you have uncovered my once blinded eyes. You have shown me your desires, your love for the unlovely, your mercy for the undeserving, your grace for the sinner. You have shown me just who I am, all of these. You have unveiled my heart. You have kindled a passion inside me that once was bare. You alone, Lord, work wonders in the hearts of your children.

My desires are not your desires. My plans are not your plans. My ways are not your ways. I can only see in front of me, when you see all around. You are invincible. You are omniscient. You are omnipresent. My mind cannot comprehend your majesty and yet you bow down, to gather this crumbled mess in the palm of your hand. You lift me up. You set me down on solid ground and reveal to me your ways. Your wondrous ways. Your beautiful ways. You make this mess into love. You string my words into comprehensible sentences. You take this life and use it for your glory. Who can do such things? What can be said of a Servant King washing these lowly feet? *Who does that?*

But you do, my Lord. You came down as the lowly babe. You laid in the lowly manger. You were nourished by your mother, taught by your father. You were adopted, dearly loved. You set the example, Servant King. You got down on your knees and carried the weight on your shoulders. You, Lord, became flesh. Perfection came down into this dirty, dusty world. Beauty came to clean the ashes. Heaven came down to set us free.

And Lord, as I pray this prayer, for eyes to see. As you answer this prayer, I see clearly things that I want to unsee. The lost. The hurting. The orphaned. The sick. The lowly. The unloved. The blind.

Lord, help the blind to see.

Strengthen the feeble hands,

steady the lees that give way;

say to those with fearful hearts,

"Be strong, do not fear;

your God will come,

he will come with vengeance;

with divine retribution he will come to save you."

Then will the eyes of the blind be opened

and the ears of the deaf unstopped.

The will the lame leap like a deer,

and the mute tongue shout for joy.

Water will gush forth in the wilderness

and streams in the desert.

Isaiah 35: 3-6

He is the Maker of heaven and earth,

the sea, and everything in them-

he remains faithful forever.

He upholds the cause of the oppressed

and gives food to the hungry.

The Lord sets prisoners free,

the Lord gives sight to the blnd,

the Lord lifts up those who are bowed down,

the Lord loves the righteous.

Psalm 146:6-8

The Neighbor

Lord, I see them now. And I cannot unsee. You have unblinded my eyes. You have given me vision that I never had. You alone have made me see. You worked through my loves. You drew me in. You broke me into a million pieces and you put me back in ways I never dreamed.

I was the neighbor no one knew. I was the one who kept to myself. Avoided eye contact. Waved when need be. I wasn't mean or cruel. I didn't avoid at all costs. I also didn't go out of my way. I didn't learn people's names. I didn't make room in my life for paths to cross. I filled every space, scheduled every minute.

Maybe I never said it out loud, Lord, but you know my thoughts. My actions spoke louder than words ever needed to. Don't disrupt my day, God. I have a plan.

I closed the curtains, locked the door. I breathed my own air. I let no soul enter in. I closed up my home and my heart. I became independent. I became solely dependent on my only one, my husband. Others were few and far between. And the crevice grew deeper and my heart nearly stopped.

Because, Lord, if I had continued down this path of seclusion, where would I be now?

Maybe, Lord, I don't need them, they need a friend. They need me? This foreign concept was the starting point for my eyes to see.

They might need me? But who am I, Lord? What do I have to offer?

And then, Lord, you unveiled the whole of your story. They do not need me. But I need them. I need the neighbor friend. The walk-beside-me-in-life friend. The long-distance friend. The come-when-I-cannot-even friend. I need the deep, soul-searching friend. The check-on-my- heart friend. The friend that needs me. The friend that pours into me. The friend that speaks truth even when it hurts. The friend that asks all the hard things from me. The friend that just sits with me.

Lord, your whole thing about the Church and the Body? The whole being, being needed and poured out and filled up? The whole community thing, fellowship? Yeah, I get it now. You did this thing and brought me here. You asked me to pray this simple prayer. Lord, give me eyes to see...your people.

My neighbor. I know them now.

My friend. I see them now.

My Church. I hear them now.

My God. You are good. Thank you for this unveiling. This blessing. This unforeseen gift. Let me never unsee your beautiful creation of the Church, the Body, your people.

Love must be sincere.

Hate what is evil;

cling to what is good.

Be devoted to one another in love.

Honor one another above yourselves.

Never be lacking in zeal,

but keep your spiritual fervor,

serving the Lord.

Be joyful in hope,

patient in affliction,

faithful in prayer.

Share with the Lord's people who are in need.

Practice hospitality.

Romans 12: 9-13

Now you are the body of Christ,

and each one of you is a part of it.

1 Corinthians 12:27

The Kid

That kid that just threw that fit? That kid that said the bad word? Taught your kid to cheat? Asked your kid to lie? That kid that bullies? Or whines? Or talks back?

Yeah, that's sometimes my kid. Sometimes it's your kid. Sometimes it's the kid down the street. Or in the classroom. Or the one getting left behind, left out, or feeling scared. Maybe dad and mom are struggling to make ends meet. Maybe they don't know how. Maybe they've just checked out. Maybe they're trying really hard. Maybe they don't know…or maybe they do?

Maybe Kid just needs some structure. Maybe Kid needs discipline. Or love. Or food. Or a stable home. Or maybe Kid just needs to care a bit. Maybe all the things are right and Kid just keeps choosing wrong? Maybe all the things are wrong and Kid just gives in?

All the needs Kid might have…we know one thing for sure, Kid needs Jesus.

Kid needs truth. Kid needs love. Kid needs boundaries. Kid needs grace.

Kid needs Jesus.

And as annoying as it may be…

As much as we want to protect our family…

As much as closing the curtains and locking the door to our hearts sounds nice…

When we are living with eyes to see, we cannot unsee them. We see the hurt, the pain, the lost. We see the child of God, not the mess of man. We see the seeds planted, not the rocky soil. We see the hope of harvest, not the wind-blown seedling. Lord, we see *you.*

Ask God who needs your love and grace today. Ask the Lord to unveil to you that one person who needs a little kindness. Ask God where to plant the seed. Don't doubt the rocky soil, God will use a willing heart.

Lord, open our eyes. Let us see you in them. Your children all around us. Your hope for weary souls. Your love for the hard ones to love. Your grace for the same-as-us sinner. Your eyes, Lord. Give us your eyes for the lost.

But Jesus called the children to him and said,

"Let the little children come to me,

and do not hinder them,

for the kingdom of God belongs to such as these.

Truly I tell you,

anyone who will not receive the kingdom of God

like a little child will never enter it."

Luke 18: 16-17

Don't you see how important children are to our Lord? Do you see their souls as Jesus sees them? His children. Dearly loved. Enter in, dear ones. Are we no better than these disciples who rebuked these children, telling them to go away from Jesus? Come, he says. There's room, always room.

And not only does he invite the children to come close, he tells the adults to be like them.

Don't be the bully, the name caller, the cheater. Be the child with heart so huge, so moldable, so ready. Be Kid with broken-heart begging to be loved. Be love. Be grace. Be kind.

Be Jesus to them.

The Enemy

Maybe enemy sounds harsh. Maybe it's not like the superhero/super villian combo we see in the movies. Maybe it's not mean girl style, dragging through mud, evil looks across the room bluntly obvious. But maybe it's a hidden agenda. Maybe it's a secret intent to make someone feel badly about themselves. Maybe it's not external at all. Maybe it's internal. Maybe it's not the other person. Maybe it's me.

Or maybe it is the other person. Maybe someone has deeply hurt you, physically or emotionally. Maybe that person shows no remorse and in your eyes deserves no forgiveness. Maybe the forgiveness isn't for them at all. Once we forgive, we live in freedom instead of bondage. Once we forgive those enemies have no hold on us. But there's more.

Once we forgive our enemies, we are supposed to take it one step further. I don't mean inviting them to live with you. I don't mean letting them continually hurt you. I don't mean letting a sinful lifestyle become an acceptable way of living. But there are ways to show love without condoning such behavior.

Let's start by love. Pure love. Jesus love. Real love. Love that is unattainable in our own strength. (Whew! I don't have to do this alone!)

"But to you who are listening I say:

Love your enemies,

do good to those who hate you,

bless those who curse you,

pray for those who mistreat you.

If someone slaps you on one cheek, turn to them the other

also.

If someone takes your coat, do not withhold your shirt from

them.

Give to everyone who asked you,

and if anyone takes what belongs to you, do not demand it

back.

Do to others as you would have them do to you.

If you love those who love you, what credit is that to you?

Even sinners love those who love them.

And if you do good to those who are good to you, what

credit is that to you?

Even sinners do that.

And if you lend to those from whom you expect repayment,

what credit is that to you?

Even sinners lend to sinners, expecting to be repaid in full.

But love you enemies, do good to them,

and lend to them without expecting to get anything back.

Then your reward will be great, and you will be children of the

Most High,

because he is kind to the ungrateful and wicked.

Be merciful, just as your Father is merciful.

Luke 6:27-36

That one person who just gets under your skin? *Pray for them.*

Seeking advice on what to do about the person who offended you? *Pray for them.*

Tempted to gossip because your hurt is so huge? *Pray for them.*

Start here, friends. Pray for eyes to see them the way God sees them. Pray for eyes to see them as dearly beloved children. Pray that they know truth. Then, seek wise, godly counsel.

Thank you, Lord we don't have to do this thing alone. Thank you for your supernatural love, grace, mercy and healing. Lord, I pray for the hurt ones reading this today. I pray for their hearts. I know your heart breaks for us. Lord, help us to feel your compassion, to trust in your love, to accept your peace and to hope in your healing. Restore us, Lord. Give us eyes to see even our enemies as your created ones. Help us to work through our emotions, our feelings, our own pain. And Lord, draw us close. Hold us. Heal us. Love us. Help us to be filled.

So we can pour out.

In Jesus Name. Amen.

Whisper

When we pray for eyes to see, we are praying for hearts to feel. We are playing for ears to listen. We are praying to know full well another's soul. We are praying to hurt when others hurt. To hunger when they hunger. To mourn when they mourn. To dance when they dance. To feel fear. To cry tears. To embrace another human's fullness; beauty and ashes.

There isn't a much greater love than a parent for a child. We feel their needs. We feed their bellies and their minds and their souls. But still in the midnight hour I find myself less patient, less understanding, less sympathetic.

So when one of my children wakes me in the night when I believe they should be sleeping, I am less responsive to his needs than when I am fully awake. In my head I know there is nothing to fear. In my mind I know he is young. Logically, there are no monsters under the bed or the yard or the room next to his. But logic gives way to his imagination and his little brain snowballs. And all the bad things that he could ever imagine flood his mind and he cannot sleep.

I drag myself into his room. Turn on some worship music, kneel beside his bed, tuck him in and pray with him. With bright blue eyes he tells me his brain will not stop even when he tries to tell it to. He tells me every time he closes his eyes the images pop into his head and he tries to get it to go away. He doesn't know why they won't. And I reassure him it's not real, but Jesus is. I say all the right words and he knows all the right things, but still he battles this real-to-him imagery.

Since praying this prayer, I feel his need more deeply. Even in my exhaustion. Even in my logic. Even in the truth. He needs me as I need the Father. He needs my reassurance as I need the Lord's. He needs my gentle spoken truth as I need God's promises.

So I meet his eyes before I turn away. I kneel down and run my fingers through his hair. I gently rub his little nose. I say to him that Jesus is near. I believe it with him. And I pray. Over him, with him and for him. I speak truth. I model truth.

I tell him to listen for the gentle whisper of our King. I tell him God is good. And as long as we are in love with Jesus, we are safe with him.

But. I do not tell him he will always be safe here on earth. I cannot promise that. It is not truth. I tell him even when we are not, God is still good. I tell him to still listen for that gentle heart whisper because Jesus never leaves us. And I tell him even when we are not safe here on earth, even when our time here is through, as long as we are in love with and believing in Jesus, then heaven is what we have to look forward to.

Heaven. The ultimate. The perfection. The hope. The forever.

Even if not…

he is still good.

Even if not…

we are safe in his arms.

Even if not…

heaven is ahead.

Rest, well my child. Whisper his name. *Jesus.* He will answer.

Even if I cannot.

Some trust in chariots and some in horses,

but we trust in the name of the Lord our God.

Psalm 20:7

In peace I will lie down and sleep,

for you alone, Lord,

make me dwell in safety.

Psalm 4:8

I will ponder all your work,

and meditate on your mighty deeds.

Your way, O God, is holy.

What god is great like our God?

Psalm 77:12,13

The Uncomfortable

When you are learning to see people the way Jesus sees them, you learn to love people the way Jesus loves them. *You meet them where they are.*

Sometimes that means you go to them.

Sometimes that means you invite them in.

Sometimes that means you get out of your comfort zone. Out of your routine. Out of your safe space.

Doing things you "don't do" and going places you "don't go" and hanging out with people who are unlike you.

I'm not so great at this, but I'm trying.

I don't love going places that are different to me, but I'll do it.

I don't love inviting people in that I don't know well, but I'll do it.

I don't love getting out of my safe space, introducing myself or making small talk, but I'm working on that welcome.

Because my heart and mind say they love people but my actions are sometimes lacking.

But who am I to say where the line is drawn? Who am I to say they should come up to me? Why shouldn't I go up to them? Say hi. Smile. Ask them how they really are. Invite them in to my life, my space or maybe join them in theirs.

It may not feel like home. But that's okay.

It may not taste like your food. But that's okay.

It may not be relaxing. Or comfortable. Or even safe. But that's okay.

Because if Jesus calls us in, he will carry us through.

Because when Jesus walked this earth, he met with people like me and you.

Because when we are in those lowly places, he bends down and lifts us up. He meets us where we are. He loves us deep. When we feel that we are sinking, he pulls us out of the muck and places us on solid ground.

Go love them hard today. Find the ones that need pulled in. Embrace the ones who are on the verge. Pray for those who hurt you. Gather your people. Make them your people. Invite them in, go to them, text them, call them. Make time for them. Just be with someone who God has placed on your heart today.

Lord, give us eyes to see that person today. Place a soul on our hearts today. Show us who needs us, who needs *you*.

Thank you, Lord, for bending down and meeting us right where we are. Thank you for showing us how and where to love people. Thank you for loving us in the most extravagant way, loving us to the cross.

In Jesus Name, Amen.

In your relationships with one another,

have the same mindset as Christ Jesus:

Who, being in very nature God,

did not consider equality with God something to be used to

his own advantage;

rather, he made himself nothing by taking the very nature of a

servant,

being made in human likeness.

And being found in appearance as a man,

he humbled himself by becoming obedient to death–

even death on a cross!

Philippians 2:5-8

While Jesus was having dinner at Levi's house,

many tax collectors and sinners were eating with him and his

disciples,

for there were many who followed him.

When teachers of the law who were Pharisees

saw him eating with sinners and tax collectors,

they asked his disciples:

"Why does he eat with tax collectors and sinners?"

On hearing this, Jesus said to them,

"It is not the healthy who need a doctor, but the sick.

I have not come to call the righteous but the sinners."

Mark 2:15-17

He lifted me out of the slimy pit,

out of the mud and mire;

he set my feet on a rock

and gave me a firm place to stand.

Psalm 40:2

Embrace

Dear Lord,

We pray today that you give us eyes to see the sameness more than the differences. We pray for hearts to embrace each other, for eyes to meet, for minds to choose to linger more than run away. Lord, we pray to remember who we are and whose we are. Help us to embrace the day and all it brings with it. The set-backs, the interruptions (opportunities), the people, the weather, the all. Thank you Lord for new days, new mercies, new starts. We give it all to you. Lift us up and set us in the place you want us. Help us to be light and love to someone today.

In Jesus Name, amen.

Ask the Lord today for one person. One person who needs love. One person to notice, to pray for, to smile at, to make a small difference in. Sometimes all it takes is a little extra tip or thank you at the coffee shop. Sometimes it's a smile in the grocery aisle. Sometimes it's telling that weary heart, "I've been there, too".

Listen for the Lord to answer. He will. He wants us to love each other. It's not hard to find these opportunities when we just simply turn our gaze from our own to-do list to the people around us.

For me, it's that mom whose life looks a little different than my own. Maybe she's single parenting, working outside the home and barely making ends meet. It's okay. She's just simply exhausted like I am. That's where we meet. In the exhaustion and weariness and just wanting to do the best we can for our kids. We are more alike than different. I embrace her. She is a mom. She is a child of God. She is just like me. And isn't that what I want, too? Someone to embrace me. See me. Love me for who I am and whose I am? Not shy away from me because of what I do or choices I've made.

Embrace the sameness today.

We are all created the same, in the image of God. We are all born helpless and sinful. We all need nurturing. We all need food and water and love.

And we all fall short. No one is born perfect and no one reaches perfection here on earth. We all sin and sin separates us from God. So big or small, visible or invisible, we are the same. Love each other in spite of it or because of it, whatever it is embrace the love the Lord provides. And give it away.

So God created mankind in his own image,

in the image of God he created them;

male and female he created them.

Genesis 1:27

This righteousness is given through faith in Jesus Christ to all

who believe.

There is no difference between Jew and Gentile,

for all have sinned and fall short of the glory of God,

and all are justified freely by his grace through the

redemption that came by Christ Jesus.

Romans 3:22-24

Changed

The worst part about coming to Jesus at such a young age is this slow and steady change. I don't have this miraculous story of terribly wrong being made right. I don't have what the world would call a transformation.

But I am changed.

I am a different person than I was before I asked the Lord to dwell in my heart. I am a different person than I was ten years ago. I am a different person than I was yesterday. The over-all growth has been slow and steady. And I am not there yet. I am changed. I am changing. I am growing. I am becoming.

As I hopefully become more like Jesus, I can see where I once was. As I intentionally carve out moments to learn, I become more aware of all I do not know. As I long to be more like my Savior, my eyes are opened to everyone around me needing this, too.

Even though my story is not the same as yours, it doesn't mean I haven't lived a sinful life. Even though I don't have a story of coming back from the brink of death or being pulled up out of addiction, doesn't mean my need for a Savior isn't just as great.

It's great. It's huge. My need to be changed daily is the same as yours. The same as my neighbors and my sisters and my children. The same as the prisoner and the beggar and the lost. The difference is always Jesus. He is what sets me apart from the ones who do not know Him.

Jesus.

Jesus made a way for me to change. To grow. To become. To be found. To see. And to give it all away. Because his love multiplies my love. His wounds took the place of my death. His resurrection makes my life new.

So as I prayed for eyes to see, God showed me greater things. I have eyes to see, not because I was so terribly wrong and bad and selfish. I have eyes to see because Jesus' love is greater. I have eyes to see not because of this prayer, but because of His mercy. I have eyes to see not because I deserve this gift or the people I can now see to love deserve it. I have eyes to see because none of us deserve it and God is good. A good gift-giver.

Thank you, Lord for changing me. Thank you for allowing me to see others for who you created them to be. Thank you, Lord, for a beautiful opportunity to see your creation, your love, your mercy. Thank you, Lord, for this gift. Amen.

Since, then, we know what it is to fear the Lord,

we try to persuade others. What we are is plain to God,

and I hope it is also plain to your conscience.

We are not trying to commend ourselves to you again,

but are giving you an opportunity to take pride in us,

so that you can answer those who take pride in what is seen

rather than in what is in the heart.

If we are "out of our mind," as some say,

it is for God;

if we are in our right mind, it is for you.

For Christ's love compels us,

because we are convinced that one died for all,

and therefore all died.

And he died for all, that those who live should no longer

live for themselves but for him who died for them

and was raised again.

So from now on we regard no one from a worldly point of view.

Though we once regarded Christ in this way,

we do so no longer.

Therefore, if anyone is in Christ,

the new creation has come;

The old is gone, the new is here!

2 Corinthians 5:11-17

Fix

I have been praying this prayer for three years now. I found it in my journal the day I decided to start this journey. I had no idea I'd be praying this consistently for so long. Or that God would change so much with this one little phrase. Or that I'd end up writing a book about it. I also had no idea how wrong I'd make it.

Wow. Somehow I've done it again. I've made it all about me. How will *I* love these people? How will *I* serve more? How will *I* be this or do that? How will I fix…and there it is. The phrase that broke me. Again.

I will not. I will never. I cannot fix anyone. Not myself or my kids or the strangers I make eye contact with. Not the girl at the check out counter or the neighbor I take cookies to. I can't fix the broken or the hurt or the hungry. How can I possibly fix them? *I am these things.*

It's pretty obvious now. I realize this may not come as a shock to you, but I will not be the one to save the world. Or my friends. Or my kids…. you get the gist.

I can be empathetic. Compassionate. Loving. Gracious. Kind. Generous. Joyful. Gentle. Humble.

But if I am not pointing them to Jesus...I may as well be apathetic. Uncaring. Unloving. Unforgiving. Unkind. Greedy. Rude. Harsh. Proud.

If I do not give them Jesus...

If I do not put off all of myself...

If I believe for a second that I am the one thing that can fix people...

I've been praying this prayer and my eyes are opened wide. But here I am doing it all wrong. I cannot be Jesus for them. Only point them to him. Only give him to them. Truth-teller. Love-gifter. Servant-leader. Gentle-friend. I am all these things, but I am not the sin-fixer. I am not the gap-filler.

Jesus is the only way. Go to him. Dear friends let me help light your way to Jesus. Let me show you the path, point you in the direction. You have to walk it.

And even if (or when) I am removed from here...life will go on. I am not needed for Jesus' plan to work. It is a privilege and a blessing to be used by him but even without me, Jesus wins.

As people around me face harsh realities. As death looms and danger lurks. As illness threatens to steal our joy. As the world feels as though it is crumbling, fix your eyes on Jesus.

Let him write your story. Don't listen to my advice, seek his counsel. Let my imperfect life, my meager words, show you the way to Jesus.

I often give myself far too much credit. I feel responsible. I feel the weight of the world, or at least my problems or my friends' problems. I feel as though I need to fix the broken, comfort the sad, feed the hungry, calm the anxious or give the best advice. What a prideful way to live.

Who am I to be that person? Only Jesus can truly feed the hungry. Only Jesus can truly heal the heart. Let me get out of the way and let Him work.

"You are the light of the world.

A town built on a hill cannot be hidden.

Neither do people light a lamp and put it under a bowl.

Instead they put it on its stand, and it gives light to everyone

the house.

In the same way, let your light shine before others,

that they may see your good deeds and glorify your Father in

heaven."

Matthew 5:14-16

Therefore, since we are surrounded by such a great cloud of

witnesses,

let us throw off everything that hingers and the sin that so

easily entangles.

And let us run with perseverance the race marked out for us,

fixing our eyes on Jesus, the pioneer and perfecter of faith.

For the joy set before him he endured the cross,

scorning its shame, and sat down at the right hand of the

throne of God.

Consider him who endured such opposition from sinners,

so that you will not grow weary and lose heart.

Hebrews 12:1-3

Jesus answered, "I am the way and the truth and the life.

No now comes to the Father except through me."

John 14:6

It's Not About Me

Maybe praying for others is how Jesus gets us over ourselves. Maybe praying for their souls, their hearts, their minds, their bodies pulls us up out of our funk and into his presence. Maybe praying for others helps us to remember the world doesn't revolve around us.

Maybe in God's mercy, what begins because we want to love others more, ends with a clear vision of his love for us.

Maybe God wants us to see ourselves for who we are, dearly loved children of God but utterly broken and in need of a Savior.

Maybe when we see ourselves in all of our depravity, we can clearly see each other in all of his love.

Maybe now we are truly beginning to see.

Today let's pray for eyes to see. Eyes to see each other, but also ourselves. Our own hearts, our own need, our own desire to be loved.

Dear Lord,

You are the Creator of all things. You make beautiful things out of dust. You re-make the broken. You give sight to the blind. And through this prayer, Lord, we've come to see you more. Our eyes are opened to how utterly broken your heart must be to see us treating each other and ourselves not as the beautiful creation you meant for us to be. Forgive us for this, Lord. You are the Potter and we am the clay. You are the Artist and we are your masterpiece. Today, dear Lord, help us to draw close to you. Help us to put you first, above all things. When we wake, Lord. When we eat, Lord, When we stress out, Lord. Keep our minds fixed on you.

Thank you Lord, for your ever-lasting patience and forever love. Amen.

Maybe you didn't know you were reading my journey. This prayer. This devotional. This is a little like my journal for this prayer. I don't have it all figured out. I don't even know what I'm doing half the time. My writing times are scattered at best Because my first priority isn't writing, although that would be awesome. But first, I feed my soul. I have time with Jesus. Then all other things. Homeschooling my children, caring for their hearts and feeding their hungry bellies. Spending time with my husband. Having coffee and conversation with a friend. Visiting my grandparents. Pouring into lives around me. It is people before projects. Hopefully, always.

But this prayer has changed my view of my time with them. I see myself as less. I see them as more. I see my time with them for them more than myself. I ask the Lord what I need to say, who I need to see. I ask Him to show me more. I ask Him how I can be His hands and feet today.

Thank you, Lord for making my blind eyes see.

Silent Pain

walk into the store. My eyes meet a small, elderly woman. She is waiting. Waiting for what? A ride? The bus? A friend? Her husband? Her child? What do those eyes hold? What led her here? What have those eyes seen?

the silent pain from seemingly unanswered prayers

the barren woman who never has her Isaac

the single friend who prayed for a spouse

the failed adoption

the unspoken, the unseen, unacknowledged

There always seems to be someone with an obvious pain or glaring loss. But we pass people each day dealing with something. And to that person, the pain is everything. The loss is real. The unexpected life I am living is just hard some days. And theirs is, too.

Today let's pray for these unseen pains, the invisible losses. They are not unseen or invisible to our Lord. He knows them. He knows them well.

Dear Lord,

Show us. You have opened our eyes. You have revealed your heart to us. You long to pour your love into all our lives. You do not play favorites. My pain and their pain, it all breaks your heart. Lord, help our hearts to seek yours. Help our minds to focus on you. Help our eyes to be fixed on you. Help our thoughts to be yours. God, we know you show up when we ask. And today we want you to know you are welcome in our lives. To show us each other. To show us who to pray for. Who to love. Who to spend a few minutes listening to. Lord, show us who to see today.

In your name. Amen.

Do not rebuke an older man harshly,

but exhort him as if he were your father.

Treat younger men as brothers, older women as sister, with

absolute purity.

Give proper recognition to those widows who are really in

need.

But if a widow has children or grandchildren,

these should learn first of all to put their religion into practice

by caring for their own family and

so repaying their parents and grandparents,

for this is pleasing to God.

The widow who is really in need and left all alone

puts her hope in God and continues night and day

to pray and to ask God for help.

1 Timothy 5:1-5

Selfish Hearts

I t's not what I need right now, or at least that's what I think. I don't want to slow down, to pause. I want to rush through bedtime. I want to have some me time. I don't want to sit here, if I'm honest. I've parented all day long.

Isn't it the same with all the things we do? Selfish hearts breed impatient parents. People who give in to their selfishness as a lifestyle, don't see other people's needs. And then we go about our day, in our own way, going our own direction. We are constantly bumping into other selfish people, blinded people, doing the exact same thing. And if you're a parent, it begins with our kids.

I have a choice to make each morning. I can force a smile when they come in to wake me up or I can make them feel like they are bothering me.

I can make them a healthy breakfast or I can let them pour their own cereal. (Both happen frequently! But it's a mindset for me.)

I can turn on music and gently guide their morning routine or I can bark orders and tell them they aren't doing it quick enough or well enough.

I set the tone for the day, for their day and my own.

Our own selfish hearts cause our eyes to be blinded. Even if you don't have children, you can set the tone for your day and help to alter others around you. Selfish hearts, grouchy attitudes, negatives thoughts, maybe that stranger at the store doesn't notice when you don't make eye contact but I bet they will notice when you do. When you smile at the lonely, when you give a little extra time or effort at work, when you go out of your way to make a meal for a family, you are serving others. But if we do all these things with the wrong heart attitude, then we are doing them wrong. If we grumble as we deliver the meal or think harsh thoughts as we walk away from the homeless, we are still doing things with a selfish heart. It's not about me. It's not about you. It's not even about the people we are seeing and serving. It's about the Lord.

Serving others with a joyful, tender heart breeds compassion in others. It changes the tone of their day and our own. It begins with more of Jesus and it leads to more of Jesus.

What simple choices can you make today to turn your tone from selfish to joyful and tender?

Who in your life gets the brunt of your selfish heart? How can you show them love today?

Dear Lord,

Thank you for a new day. Thank you for the sun coming up each morning and the promise of new mercies and fresh starts. We pray today that you break our selfish hearts. Break them open and fill them with your joy and your compassion and your tenderness. Show us who you want us to serve today. Help us Lord, to be filled with your love and to let it overflow into our everyday, mundane tasks we set out to accomplish today. We praise you for who you are, the breaker and healer of hearts.

In Jesus name, amen.

You, my brothers and sisters, were called to be free.
But do not use your freedom to indulge the flesh;
rather, serve one another humbly in love.
For the entire law is fulfilled in keeping this one command;
"Love your neighbor as yourself."

Galatians 5:13-14

Breaking Hearts

She gets up in the night. Her bed is wet…again. I know she'll be discouraged and frustrated tomorrow. Plus the lack of sleep puts an irritable spin on her day.

His eyes tell me things. He asks questions most nine-year-olds don't. He doesn't know the answers. He repeats himself a lot. He needs me to reassure him. Maybe he just isn't really listening well. Maybe his mind is wandering to a place where he didn't know the answer to where he was going or what was next or if there was even food for another meal.

I catch my breath. I try to keep the tears from falling, but it's just too much. I choke them back by not singing the words that everyone around me in church are singing. I can't. Because right now, to me, death does sting. I lost my son. Why don't I ever just say the words out loud, "he died, my son is dead". Because it stings. It's salt in an open wound. I think it. Inside my head, I scream it. My son lost his parents. My daughter, too. My children lost their brother. This world is so broken.

How good it is to sing praises to our God,

how pleasant and fitting to praise him!

The Lord builds up Jerusalem;

he gathers the exiles of Israel.

He heals the brokenhearted

and binds up their wounds.

He determines the number of the stars

and calls them each by name.

Great is out Lord and might in power;

his understanding has no limit.

The Lord sustains the humble

but casts the wicked to the ground.

Sing to the Lord with grateful praise;

make music to our God on the harp.

Psalm 147:1-7

We don't have to look far to see the broken. But sometimes I have to remember to look past myself. And when our eyes are open to see people, we also see the broken. We feel the broken. We are the broken. We are broken for our children, for death, for others around us.

What do we do with our broken hearts?

We cannot hide from them or run away. Burying our hurt will cause it to simmer in our hearts. Turning our eyes away from other's broken-hearts is not love. We embrace the broken. We cling to his promises. We love them the best we can and trust Jesus to do the rest.

In my life, he has given the orphan a home. He has fed the hungry. He hs brought joy in the mourning. He has shown me glimpses of the beautiful, perfect redemption to come.

Don't shy away from the broken today. Pray to see more of it. And then trust the Lord to redeem it. Maybe not today or tomorrow or on this earth. But one day. One day is coming…

Ask

I have prayed this prayer. I have purposefully set time aside. I have learned that loving people, seeing people the way Jesus sees them is a life-long journey. It's not a lesson to be learned and checked off the list. It's a practice. A discipline.

It's humbling and it's hard. It's beautiful and it's messy.

If we are to see with eyes wide open but never get up to do anything, it's the same as a selfish heart. Even unbelievers can see people. Even unbelievers can be kind and generous and loving.

The Lord has given us great freedom. We can love each other well because it's not our responsibility to make their choices for them. We can love each other well because he loves us in abundance. We just have to ask.

Oh my goodness. We are free. It's so simple.

I ask.

He answers.

I ask.

He fills me up.

I ask.

He pours out.

I ask.

He sustains.

I ask.

He gives.

I ask.

He provides.

I ask.

He makes me see.

And through it all, *He is good.*

Even when I see the most unlovely of things. The things that keep me up at night. The things that break my heart. I can rest well because I know they break his heart, too. This is not how it was meant to be. This is not the best. This is not the end.

"I will make all things new," he promises. (from Revelation 21:5 and Isaiah 43:19) He sees it, too. This imperfect world and selfish hearts and blinded eyes. He sees it, too. His heart breaks even more than mine.

He feels it all. He heals it all…eventually.

Hang on, dear heart. You may be broken now, but beautiful things will come out of it.

Hang on, dear heart. You may feel overwhelmed and burdened with the weight of the world. But it is not yours to carry. Give it back to God. He was. He is. He is to come. There is nothing that will surprise him or overwhelm him or outlast him.

Dear Lord,

Seeing is such a gift and a burden. Help us to know how to give it all to you today, The weight of the world is not ours to carry. Thank you for being the one to carry it all. Thank you for your promise of redemption and restoration and new things. Thank you for loving us so well.

In Jesus name, amen.

"Ask and it will be given to you;

seek and you will find;

knock and the door will be opened to you.

For everyone who asks receives;

the one who seeks finds;

and to the one who knocks, the door will be opened."

Matthew 7:7-8

"Come to me, all you who are weary and burdened, and I will

give you rest.

Take my yoke upon you and learn from me, for I am gentle

and humble in heart, and you will find rest for your souls.

For my yoke is easy and my burden is light."

Matthew 11:28-30

Thank you for praying this prayer. For enduring this journey. For loving enough to get to this point. I look forward to many, many more years of growing closer to Christ. I hope and pray you do, too.

Now, let's go, with unblinded eyes, love God and love people.

-Tiffany

Made in the USA
Middletown, DE
27 January 2021

32501259R00086